Somerset County MEMORIES
THE EARLY YEARS

Introductions by James A. Flachsenhaar
Edited by Andrea L. Aleff and Paul C. Grzella

Presented by

Courier News
Your news, every day.

ACKNOWLEDGMENTS

The *Courier News* is pleased to present *Somerset County Memories ~ The Early Years*.

This unique pictorial book is not a publication of just the *Courier News,* however. It is the result of contributions made by many people and organizations.

We are all indebted, first of all, to those early residents of Somerset County who captured their times in photographs and provided us with a glimpse into their lives. And, secondly, we thank the many individuals who are committed to preserving our history in libraries, archives and personal collections around the county.

We are pleased to acknowledge the generous contribution of time and photos from the following:

Bernardsville Public Library

Clarence Dillon Public Library

Franklin Township Public Library

Hillsborough Reformed Church at Millstone

The Historical Society of the Somerset Hills

Millstone Historic District Commission

North Plainfield Exempt Firemen's Association Museum

Rocky Hill Community Group

Somerset County Historical Society

Van Harlingen Historical Society

Warren Township Historical Society

TABLE OF CONTENTS

FOREWORD

It was only a moment ago – in the long view of history – that our vistas were forested, our bridges were wooden and horses competed with cars for rights-of-way on packed-dirt roads.

And anyone with a camera, it seemed, loved to capture even the simplest images; our turn-of-the-century scrapbook is filled with indelible scenes of intersections, rivers and railroad tracks.

These pictures are how we remember Somerville and Raritan, Basking Ridge and Rocky Hill, Millstone and Far Hills. In our mind's eye it is satisfying to superimpose these old images on the locations as they exist today, and marvel at how far we have come. But it's not always easy. Check "Road to Morristown from Basking Ridge" on Page 11, for instance. Could you find that bend in the road today?

These are more than postcards, though. They illuminate the way we lived not so long ago. Look closer and you'll see laundry drying on the backyard line, hats for every occasion and men wearing – what else? – dress suits for a spin on the bicycle.

As Somerset County has grown up, the *Courier News* has been telling its story. The result of an 1894 merger between *The Evening News* (established in 1884) and the *Plainfield Courier* (1891), the *Courier News* always has been a part of the lives of the people who live and work in Somerset County. Now, as then, our pages include the events that matter – from birth announcements to high school graduations, from baseball scores to wedding announcements.

As Somerset County has changed, we have, too. We have progressed from early printing-press technology to full-color offset printing. But our commitment to local news, to honesty and accuracy, and to friendly customer service, remains the same.

We are as pleased to bring you this book of early memories of Somerset County as we are to deliver the most complete Somerset County newspaper to your home every day.

Charles W. Nutt
President and Publisher

VIEWS AROUND THE COUNTY

My, how we've grown.
In a century, Somerset County has been transformed from sleepy, bucolic pastures and rudimentary wood-frame towns to an economic and residential hub striving to strike a balance between relentless development and quality of life.

But these photographs from the late 1800s and early 1900s remind us how simple and beautiful the early years were. The "skyline" of Far Hills, for instance, resembled that of a Midwest prairie town. Basking Ridge and Martinsville evoked the changeless, graceful repose of rural Vermont. Gaze long enough, and the old canal in Raritan reinterprets itself in the short-strokes mastery of the Impressionists.

In both abstract and physical terms, churches were at the center of community life. As for transportation, either a horse or new-fangled automobile would do. And if you stood on any Main Street and turned in a 360-degree circle, you'd see porches and picket fences, wooden bridges and grist mills, delivery buggies and rickety wooden hotels, and – perhaps – the town's first telephone polls.

This was Somerset County, whose patriotism and architecture and rutted streets were lovingly documented by its first photographers.

Looking up Main Street in Millstone, early 1900s. *Courtesy Hazel Dickinson*

Kingston, where three counties meet: Somerset, Middlesex and Mercer, 1884. Kingston also straddles three municipalities. The northernmost tip is in Franklin Township, Somerset County. The largest portion of Kingston is in South Brunswick, Middlesex County. The Princeton part of Kingston is in Mercer County. *Courtesy Franklin Township Public Library*

The old canal, Raritan, late 1800s. *Courtesy Somerset County Historical Society*

Delaware and Raritan Canal snakes through Millstone River Valley in Central Jersey. Barges, steamboats and yachts once traveled on this stretch of the canal, between Kingston and Rocky Hill. *Courtesy Rocky Hill Community Group*

Road leading to Martinsville. *Courtesy Somerset County Historical Society*

Washington Street, Rocky Hill, late 1800s. *Courtesy Rocky Hill Community Group*

Water tower, Raritan, late 1800s. *Courtesy Somerset County Historical Society*

Looking down Main Street, Millstone, circa 1900. *Courtesy Hazel Dickinson*

Far Hills, late 1800s.
Courtesy Clarence Dillon Public Library

Livingston Avenue, East Millstone, circa 1900. *Courtesy Hazel Dickinson*

Franklin Township section of Kingston, circa 1901. *Courtesy Franklin Township Public Library*

The bridge that connected Millstone with East Millstone, circa 1900. *Courtesy Hazel Dickinson*

The Spring, Basking Ridge, circa 1905. *Courtesy The Historical Society of the Somerset Hills*

Market Street, East Millstone, circa 1900. *Courtesy Hazel Dickinson*

Corner of Main Street and Mount Avenue, Pluckemin, circa 1905. *Courtesy The Historical Society of the Somerset Hills*

A small commercial center was established in the village of East Millstone in 1834, when the Delaware and Raritan Canal opened. East Millstone continued to prosper after the Millstone and New Brunswick Railroad opened in 1854. The village loosened its ties to Franklin Township in 1873 and became a separate town. In 1949, the village rejoined Franklin Township.

Courtesy Franklin Township Public Library

Main Street looking east, Martinsville, circa 1905. *Courtesy Somerset County Historical Society*

Finley Avenue, showing Dayton's Hall and R.A. Henry's residence, Basking Ridge. *Courtesy The Historical Society of the Somerset Hills*

Main Street, Basking Ridge, early 1900s. *Courtesy The Historical Society of the Somerset Hills*

Road to Morristown from Basking Ridge. *Courtesy The Historical Society of the Somerset Hills*

Main Street, Pluckemin, circa 1905. *Courtesy The Historical Society of the Somerset Hills*

View of Kingston, 1906. Fisk's grocery store is on the left, the lock tender's house and gristmill are in the center rear and the Hoffman House Hotel is on the right. *Courtesy Franklin Township Public Library*

Franklin Park, 1905. After the first Somerset County Courthouse was built, Six Mile Run (Franklin Park) was a hub of county activity for almost a quarter of a century. When the courthouse burned in 1737, the county seat was moved to Millstone. *Courtesy Franklin Township Public Library*

Main Street, Basking Ridge, circa 1905. *Courtesy The Historical Society of the Somerset Hills*

A view of Market Street in East Millstone with the town's first automobile, owned by Charles Van Nostrand, circa 1907. The automobile was a Stanley Steamer. George Pace, a New Jersey assemblyman and owner of Pace's Hotel, joined Van Nostrand for the ride. *Courtesy Franklin Township Public Library*

Bird's-eye view of Pottersville, 1906. *Courtesy Clarence Dillon Public Library*

Old covered bridge, South Branch, June 30, 1908. *Courtesy Somerset County Historical Society*

Olcott Avenue, Middlebush, 1908. Middlebush was one of the first areas of Franklin to receive telephone service. *Courtesy Franklin Township Public Library*

Market Street, East Millstone, 1908. *Courtesy Franklin Township Public Library*

Main Street, Somerville, circa 1911. *Courtesy Somerville Public Library*

COMMERCE & INDUSTRY

Although modern Somerset County has been described as the buckle of Central Jersey's "Wealth Belt," 100 years ago it was anything but bustling. Forget mall shopping; you had to look hard to find two stores side-by-side.

Communities with large populations, or those where the wealthy built homes – among them Somerville, Bernardsville and Bound Brook – were the first to establish an industrial base and business districts. With the main growth industry being growth itself, it's no surprise that banks, mills, hardware stores and lumberyards dominated the early landscape. Blacksmiths, too, were widespread before horses were supplanted by automobiles.

Want a "Snappy Boy" wagon for your children? Try the hardware store in Bernardsville. A room for the night? There were hotels in Bernardsville, Pottersville (a neighborhood of Bedminster), Bound Brook, Rocky Hill, Franklin Park and Somerville, among other places.

As you'll see on the following pages, most of our early businesses survive only as grainy, black-and-white images. In some cases, such as Somerville's First National Bank and Gaston Building, the businesses are defunct but the buildings remain. And in a handful of happy instances – the Bernards Inn in Bernardsville, the quarry at Chimney Rock, Bridgewater and the Trap Rock Quarry in Franklin – it's been business as usual for decades.

Gianquitti's Hardware Store, Bernardsville, early 1900s. *Courtesy Bernardsville Public Library*

Gernert's Store on Main Street, Somerville, circa 1885. It was a general store offering a variety of stock, including children's items such as Champion wagons, go-carts, tricycles and toys. *Courtesy Somerville Public Library*

The Old Stone Hotel in Bernardsville was built by John Bunn in 1849. John Beck was the first proprietor. *Courtesy Bernardsville Public Library*

A blacksmith shop was located at the intersection of Province Line Road and New Brunswick-Lambertville Turnpike at Stoutsburg, also known as Dogtown. It was owned and operated by William A. Simmins from 1852-1915. It was demolished in 1915. The post office also was housed in this building. Photo, 1882. *Courtesy Somerset County Historical Society*

Pottersville Hotel was built in 1889 by Henry "Whisky Hank" Fleming when the Rockaway Valley Railroad came to town. *Courtesy Clarence Dillon Public Library*

Interior of the Six Mile Run Blacksmith Shop, Franklin Township, late 1800s. *Courtesy Somerset County Historical Society*

Stone crusher at Chimney Rock, above Bound Brook, late 1800s.
Courtesy Somerset County Historical Society

Basket factory, Pottersville, late 1800s. *Courtesy Somerset County Historical Society*

Haelig's Hotel, Chimney Rock, late 1800s. *Courtesy Somerset County Historical Society*

Excelsior Terra Cotta Factory, located on more than 100 acres next to the Delaware and Raritan Canal and the railroad, 1897. Workers used a floating barrel footbridge across the canal (far left) to go to Rocky Hill. In 1907, this site became the Atlantic Terra Cotta Factory. *Courtesy Rocky Hill Community Group*

Cutting ice on Watchung Lake. *Courtesy Somerset County Historical Society*

Somerville Woolen Mill, late 1800s. *Courtesy Somerset County Historical Society*

E.B. Bergen Grocer, late 1800s. *Courtesy Van Harlingen Historical Society*

Peter Freiday, a blacksmith, was the grandson of George Freiday, Warren. Photo, circa 1900. *Courtesy Warren Township Historical Society*

Liddy Brothers Meats, Groceries and Provisions Store, Bernardsville, early 1900s. From left to right: Frank Liddy, Thomas Liddy, Jr., unidentified, _____ Cavanaugh, Mary Liddy, Martin Liddy, unidentified, unidentified. *Courtesy Bernardsville Public Library*

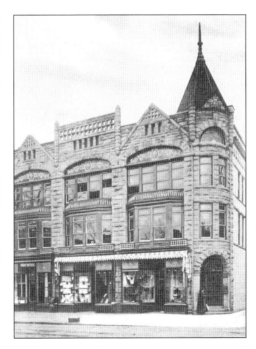

Gaston Building, Somerville, circa 1900. This structure was built on the corner of Main and Maple streets by Senator Lewis Thompson in 1891. It became known locally as "*the store occupying the ground floor.*" In addition to the department store, the building housed the Somerville Post Office around 1900. *Courtesy Somerset County Historical Society*

Bernards Inn, Bernardsville, early 1900s. *Courtesy Bernardsville Public Library*

Newton O. Dunster Livery and Boarding Stable, Somerville, early 1900s.
Courtesy Somerset County Historical Society

Rocky Hill Inn, a fashionable summer excursion stop-off for city residents until the 1930s. *Courtesy Rocky Hill Community Group*

L.H. Nuse Horse-shoeing and Jobbing, Bernardsville, early 1900s. *Courtesy Bernardsville Public Library*

David Stewart's tavern on Somerset Street in what is now Watchung, the site of Warren's first township committee meeting on April 14, 1806. *Courtesy Warren Township Historical Society*

Bolmer Motors, one of the first car dealers in the area, on East Main Street, Bound Brook. The gentlemen in the photo also repaired cars. Early 1900s. *Courtesy Somerset County Historical Society*

A bank on the corner of Bridge and Main streets in Somerville has been a landmark since the middle 1800s. This structure, with its iron grates, was constructed on this corner first. *Courtesy Somerville Public Library*

First National Bank at Maple and Main, Somerville, 1901. The building was designed by architect George Post of the New York Stock Exchange and was built in 1901. The first Main Street offices of the Unionist Gazette Book and Job Printing stood next door. *Courtesy Somerville Public Library*

Jacob Reinmann, who owned 88 acres on Reinman Road, hauled timber from Warren to railroad flat cars in Millington. The poles were transported to New York City and used to build the city's piers. Reinmann also ran a stagecoach that brought summer boarders to Warren from the railroad depot in Plainfield. Reinmann's property was sold in 1928 and divided into building lots. Plainfield Gardens is the name of his farm today. *Courtesy Warren Township Historical Society*

Two Somerset County businessmen discuss matters in a gas-lit office believed to be an insurance firm, circa 1900. *Courtesy Somerset County Historical Society*

Funeral home, Millstone, 1886-1924. William C. Kitchen was the funeral director, circa 1900. *Courtesy Hazel Dickinson*

Luther Anthony's General Store located at the corner of Laurel Avenue and Main Street (Route 27), Kingston, July 4, 1904. *Courtesy Franklin Township Public Library*

Wheelwright Peter S. DeHart (right) and his son John stand in the doorway of Peter's wheelwright shop at Three Mile Run, 1904. *Courtesy Franklin Township Public Library*

Franklin's Trap Rock Quarry, early 1900s. This quarry in southern Franklin has been in operation since before the 1850s and has had several names. During the 1860s, it produced paving block used to surface miles of streets in Jersey City and Newark. At the time of this photo, it was known as the Delaware River Quarry Company. In recent years rock from this quarry was used to construct the New Jersey Turnpike. *Courtesy Franklin Township Public Library*

Beekman's Hotel, Franklin Park, 1904. This hotel was built by Christopher Columbus Beekman on land that had been occupied by taverns since Colonial times. *Courtesy Franklin Township Public Library*

Somerset Inn, Bernardsville, circa 1905. *Courtesy Clarence Dillon Public Library*

D & R Canal in Zarephath, circa 1903. *Courtesy Somerset County Historical Society*

Van Dorn's Mill, Basking Ridge. *Courtesy The Historical Society of the Somerset Hills*

Bedminster Hotel, circa 1905. *Courtesy The Historical Society of the Somerset Hills*

Pleasant Valley Mill, circa 1906. *Courtesy The Historical Society of the Somerset Hills*

Owner and Postmaster Charles C. Hullfish at his desk in Hull-fish's Store, located on the South Brunswick side of Route 27 in Franklin Park, 1905. Just over the Somerset County border, it was also the post office and a favorite meeting place for villag-ers. *Courtesy Franklin Township Public Library*

C. C. Hullfish store in Franklin Park, September 1906. Seated on the front steps from left: John Mershon, Cornelius VanDeveer, James Hullfish, Charles C. Hullfish and the store clerk, Pierson. Lester Hullfish is on the bicycle. *Courtesy Franklin Township Public Library*

Mrs. Zimmermann's Beer Wagon from New Brunswick in front of the hotel in Franklin Park, June 28, 1906. *Courtesy Franklin Township Public Library*

Somerset Hospital, Somerville, in its first building. *Courtesy Somerville Public Library*

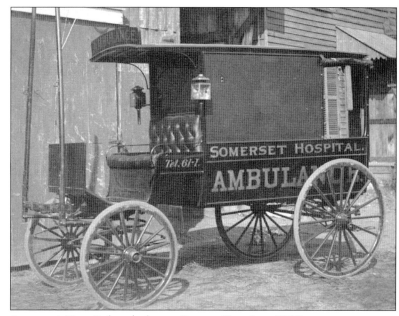

Somerset Hospital ambulance, Somerville, circa 1905. *Courtesy Somerville Public Library*

Thomas Building, Somerville, circa 1906. *Courtesy Somerville Public Library*

Ten Eyck Hotel, Somerville, circa 1906. *Courtesy Somerville Public Library*

Allen's Auditorium, Borough of Peapack, circa 1907. *Courtesy The Historical Society of the Somerset Hills*

Directors' Room, First National Bank, Somerville, 1908. *Courtesy Somerville Public Library*

King George Inn was built in the 1700s in Warren. In 1873, Jacob Blimm, then the proprietor, advertised a stage line from Plainfield to Mount Bethel. Josephine Schaeffer, who sang at the Metropolitan Opera, lived here in the 1880s. In 1909, the inn was frequented by city residents who came to enjoy the country air. Photo, 1909. *Courtesy Warren Township Historical Society*

Cooper's Store, East Millstone, circa 1909. *Courtesy Franklin Township Public Library*

Albert T. Lewis' store at 125-127 Washington Street, Rocky Hill. Albert's brother, I. Morgan Lewis, added a post office next to the store after President Woodrow Wilson appointed him postmaster in 1914. *Courtesy Rocky Hill Community Group*

Washington House and W.E. Tunis Store, Basking Ridge. *Courtesy The Historical Society of the Somerset Hills*

A sawmill and lumberyard on the boat basin of the Delaware and Raritan Canal at Rocky Hill was operated by the Stryker family. *Courtesy Rocky Hill Community Group*

Martinsville Inn, circa 1910. *Courtesy Somerset County Historical Society*

Bachmann and Van Tine Central Cash Grocers, Somerville, 1910. This market specialized in fresh produce. Wearing a cap, tie and apron, Van Tine is ready to help his customers. He was killed in World War I. *Courtesy Somerville Public Library*

Commercial Hotel, Somerville, circa 1910. *Courtesy Somerville Public Library*

Somerville Iron Works on James Street, circa 1910. It was founded in 1905 and employed 200 men, who made cast-iron stoves, sewer covers, soil pipes and lawn mowers. *Courtesy Somerville Public Library*

Garretson Automobile and Cycle Company on Main Street in Somerville, circa 1911. *Courtesy Somerville Public Library*

Somerset Trust Company, once the First National Bank, and Mrs. Baunngartner's Hat Shop, Somerville, circa 1911. *Courtesy Somerville Public Library*

Old Regent Theatre, Somerville, circa 1911. *Courtesy Somerville Public Library*

Shippers at the Atlantic Terra Cotta Factory crate and load decorative pieces. At that time it was advertised that the process from drawing board to destination took no more than eight weeks. *Courtesy Rocky Hill Community Group*

SCHOOLS & EDUCATION

Like schools today, Somerset County's earliest schools focused on reading, writing and arithmetic. They did not, it seems, have any problem with classroom overcrowding or inappropriate attire. Nor is there much evidence of disruptive student behavior; in class photos on the following pages, the students are hardly smiling.

Education at the turn of the century was a local affair. Communities built their own schools and hired their own teachers, often holding classes in structures that resembled houses more than modern schools. Curriculum was based on tradition, not state mandates.

Students – especially in the higher grades – dressed for the occasion, despite having to walk a few miles daily to get back and forth between home and school. Parental involvement was a given, desks had inkwells and teachers ruled with an iron hand.

What, you might wonder, was discussed for current events? Probably events such as the 1904 opening of the New York City subway system (linking City Hall and Canal Street), the Russian Revolution, Norway's separation from Sweden and President Theodore Roosevelt's mediation of the end of the war between Russia and Japan – topics supplanted in time by World War I, Prohibition and the Crash of '29.

Basking Ridge School, first and second grades, 1909. *Courtesy The Historical Society of the Somerset Hills*

Warrenville schoolhouse at 67 Mount Bethel Road was built in 1847 to replace an earlier school erected prior to the Revolution. Now a private home, the building retains the carved remnants of students' names and initials on its window frames.
Courtesy Warren Township Historical Society

Burnt Mills School classroom, Pluckemin, late 1800s. *Courtesy Clarence Dillon Public Library*

Rocky Hill School children, late 1800s. Miss Johnson was one of the teachers. *Courtesy Rocky Hill Community Group*

Old School, Bridgewater Township, located on Washington Valley Road. *Courtesy Somerset County Historical Society*

Rocky Hill School was built in 1848 and operated until a new school was built in 1908. It was the first public school in town. William S. Durling bought this school and property in 1914 and turned the structure into a residence. *Courtesy Rocky Hill Community Group*

The original Main Street School, Manville, circa 1900. Bernhard Meyer, Jr. is in front holding the bat. *Courtesy Marian Meyer*

The old Smalleytown School in Warren, circa 1900. This school was built of fieldstone circa 1800. The large elm was planted as "guardian" of the pupils who studied there in 1842, the same year the township acquired the land. The building to the left was a stagecoach stop around 1790. *Courtesy Warren Township Historical Society*

Interior of a Franklin Township Schoolhouse, early 1900s. The schools were located approximately three miles apart – the distance a school child could be expected to walk or ride a horse each day. *Courtesy Franklin Township Public Library*

Pottersville School children, early 1900s. *Courtesy Bernardsville Public Library*

Middlebush Schoolhouse No. 5 was built in 1859. The school stood originally in back of the Reformed Church. The second floor was used for Sunday school and prayer meetings. In 1907, the four upper grades were moved upstairs, making it Franklin's first two-room schoolhouse. In 1916, the building was moved across the street and used as a private residence.
Courtesy Franklin Township Public Library

Schoolhouse in Franklin Park, circa 1904. *Courtesy Franklin Township Public Library*

Far Hills School, October 1905. *Courtesy Clarence Dillon Public Library*

Horse-drawn school buses in front of Olcott School, Bernardsville, 1908. *Courtesy Bernardsville Public Library*

Students from Middlebush Schoolhouse No. 5, circa 1910. *Courtesy Franklin Township Public Library*

Springdale School students, Warren Township, circa 1913. *Courtesy Warren Township Historical Society*

Edmund E. Sage, teacher, and students from the South Stirling School in Warren from 1911-1916. Photo, circa 1914. *Courtesy Warren Township Historical Society*

Maple Avenue School eighth grade, November 1909. *Courtesy Somerset Hills Historical Society*

Bernards High School
students, 1913.

Courtesy Bernardsville Public Library

Public school, Pea-
pack, early 1900s.

*Courtesy The Historical
Society of the Somerset Hills*

Classroom of Basking Ridge School, third and fourth grades. *Courtesy The Historical Society of the Somerset Hills*

Washington School, Bound Brook, circa 1915. *Courtesy Somerset County Historical Society*

Children pose in front of the St. Elizabeth School, Bernardsville, early 1900s. *Courtesy Bernardsville Public Library*

Mount Bethel School class, Warren, 1914. *Courtesy Warren Township Historical Society*

SOCIETY

In the early 1900s, families enjoyed little free time. There was more than enough work and household chores to go around for adults and children alike. Not surprisingly, attending Sunday services – and greeting friends and neighbors afterward – was often the only social event of the week.

From picnics to parades, from baptisms to weddings to funerals, our houses of worship – and the sense of community they provided – were the religious and social backbone of Somerset County. The East Millstone Reformed Church Centennial Celebration on October 9, 1905, for instance, drew a crowd and provided the perfect opportunity for conversation and camaraderie. The same was true for the "Early Harvest Home" picnic, held on the front lawn of the Hillsborough Reformed Church.

Throughout Somerset County, churches remained a part of society after the congregation replaced them, typically with new, larger structures. Old houses of worship were often purchased, dismantled and reassembled elsewhere as barns, businesses and factories. Often, when the congregation moved to a new location, the old structures were sold and converted into private residences, restaurants and businesses.

Ultimately, our houses of worship are among the most enduring links to the past. No other buildings in our communities look as much the same now as they did then.

First Baptist Church, High Street, Somerville, 1906. It was designed by Asa Dilta, a local builder who erected many New Jersey churches. *Courtesy Somerville Public Library*

Six Mile Run Dutch
Reformed Church in
Franklin Park, circa 1870.
*Courtesy Somerset County
Historical Society*

Chimney Rock Cha-
pel in Bridgewater,
December 1897.
*Courtesy Somerset County
Historical Society*

Bedminster Reformed Church, third building. *Courtesy Clarence Dillon Public Library*

Interior of the Chimney Rock Chapel, 1893. *Courtesy Somerset County Historical Society*

Second church building of the Dutch Reformed Church of Bedminster, built in 1818. It stood on Somerville Road, near the present cemetery, and was destroyed by high winds in 1896 while being moved to a new location. *Courtesy Bernardsville Public Library*

Hillsborough Reformed Church, Millstone, early 1900s. *Courtesy Hazel Dickinson*

Trinity Episcopal Church, on the corner of Crescent Avenue and Park Avenue (which was then Mount Street), Rocky Hill. *Courtesy Rocky Hill Community Group*

Picnic "Early Harvest Home" on the front lawn of the Hillsborough Reformed Church. *Courtesy Hillsborough Reformed Church at Millstone*

Methodist Church, Gladstone, founded in 1838. *Courtesy The Historical Society of the Somerset Hills*

Rocky Hill Dutch Reformed Church, with parsonage on the left. Prior to its construction, parishioners gathered on Saturdays for Sunday School in a nearby barn or at the old schoolhouse and attended church on Sunday in Harlingen. *Courtesy Rocky Hill Community Group*

Reformed Church, Peapack, circa 1906. *Courtesy The Historical Society of the Somerset Hills*

St. Mark's Episcopal Church, Basking Ridge. *Courtesy The Historical Society of the Somerset Hills*

St. Elizabeth Catholic Church, Far Hills, early 1900s. *Courtesy Clarence Dillon Public Library*

Middlebush Church, 1900. *Courtesy Hazel Dickinson*

Reformed Church, Middlebush. *Courtesy Somerset County Historical Society*

Pluckemin Presbyterian Church, circa 1905. *Courtesy The Historical Society of the Somerset Hills*

Presbyterian Church and Historic Oak Tree, Basking Ridge, circa 1900. The origin of this church dates to 1702. The present structure was built in 1839 on the site of a former one, built in 1719 where the Log Church stood. The Historic Oak is estimated at 400 years old. Its branches extend 130 feet from tip to tip and its trunk, to 23 feet, 7 inches in circumference. During the Revolutionary War, George Washington ate dinner beneath this tree. *Courtesy The Historical Society of the Somerset Hills*

Warren's Baptist Meeting House was built in 1761 on Quibbletown Gap Road (Old Church Road), then disassembled and moved to its present site in 1785. It is listed on the National Register of Historic Places. Photo, circa 1910. *Courtesy Warren Township Historical Society*

Methodist Episcopal Church, Gladstone, circa 1905. *Courtesy Clarence Dillon Public Library*

Methodist Episcopal Church on West High Street, Somerville, 1906. *Courtesy Somerville Public Library*

East Millstone Reformed Church Centennial Celebration, October 9, 1905. *Courtesy Hillsborough Reformed Church at Millstone*

PUBLIC SERVICE

It wasn't so long ago that fire, not crime, was the most significant public-safety issue in Somerset County. To be in public service around the turn of the century typically meant being a fireman. And when you weren't fighting fires, it seems, you were posing proudly, with all your equipment, for photographs.

Fireman also rode a technological wave, of sorts, as gas-powered fire trucks replaced horse-drawn fire wagons in the early 1900s. For a time, departments in Basking Ridge, Bernardsville, Somerville and other communities had both varieties, as these pictures show.

Later, as World War I began to grip the world, Somerset County communities trained local militias, prepared their sons for military service and held parades to demonstrate their patriotism.

The county was also no stranger to politics, from appearances of the county freeholders at local events to visits by presidents and would-be presidents at political rallies. Alton B. Parker and Henry Gassaway Davis, losers to Theodore Roosevelt in 1904, drew a crowd as they campaigned in Olcott Square in Bernardsville. Roosevelt himself visited in 1912 – running unsuccessfully for president on the independent Bull Moose ticket – and raised his mighty voice from the steps of the Somerset Courthouse.

North Plainfield Fire Department in the late 1800s. *Courtesy North Plainfield Exempt Firemen's Association Museum*

Members of Rocky Hill Hook and Ladder Company No. 1 pose in front of the old firehouse behind Voorhees Hall on Crescent Avenue, Rocky Hill. *Courtesy Rocky Hill Community Group*

The first firehouse in the Old Stone Hotel Barn, Bernardsville, circa 1898. *Courtesy Bernardsville Public Library*

Members of Somerville Fire Department's Engine Company No. 3 in front of their firehouse, early 1900s. *Courtesy Somerset County Historical Society*

Horse-drawn apparatus with Prince and Duke in harness, Bernardsville Company, early 1900s. *Courtesy Bernardsville Public Library*

Volunteer members of Warren Engine Company No. 1 in front of their fire house, circa 1895. *Courtesy North Plainfield Exempt Firemen's Association Museum*

Volunteer members of Warren Engine Company No. 1 line up for inspection, circa 1895. *Courtesy North Plainfield Exempt Firemen's Association Museum*

Bernardsville Fire Company, early 1900s. *Courtesy Bernardsville Public Library*

Somerville Fire Company, late 1800s. *Courtesy Somerset County Historical Society*

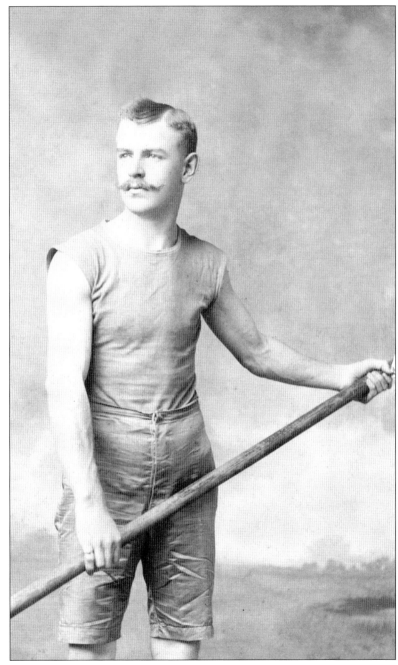

George A. Casey, fireman in Bernardsville, circa 1900. *Courtesy Bernardsville Public Library*

Bernardsville fire chief, circa 1908. *Courtesy Bernardsville Public Library*

Gladstone's first fire truck rolls down Main Street, circa 1900. *Courtesy The Historical Society of the Somerset Hills*

The first firehouse in Far Hills, early 1900s. *Courtesy Clarence Dillon Public Library*

West End fireman, Somerville, holds "Old Harry's" reins. *Courtesy Somerville Public Library*

Central Hook and Ladder Company on Division Street, Somerville, early 1900s. *Courtesy Somerville Public Library*

Somerville Engine Company ready for a parade, circa 1905. *Courtesy Somerset County Historical Society*

Members of Basking Ridge Fire Company No. 1 pause before Old Oak Tree, 1910. *Courtesy The Historical Society of the Somerset Hills*

Bernardsville Fire Company No. 1 truck, 1901. This photo was taken on Mill Street looking toward the Square in Bernardsville. *Courtesy Bernardsville Public Library*

Basking Ridge Fire Company No. 1. *Courtesy The Historical Society of the Somerset Hills*

West End Hose Company fire truck, Somerville. *Courtesy Somerville Public Library*

Bernardsville fire truck, early 1900s. *Courtesy Bernardsville Public Library*

Members of Basking Ridge Fire Company No. 1 show off their new fire car, circa 1910. *Courtesy The Historical Society of the Somerset Hills*

Union Hook and Ladder Company No. 1, Far Hills, 1915. *Courtesy Clarence Dillon Public Library*

Somerset County Freeholders, circa 1900. William John Logan is second from the right. *Courtesy Marian Meyer*

George Washington's Headquarters, Rocky Hill, 1896.
Courtesy Somerset County Historical Society

The old Somerset County Courthouse, Somerville, was demolished in the early 1900s to make way for a new structure. *Courtesy Somerset County Historical Society*

Somerset County Courthouse, completed in 1906. *Courtesy Somerset County Historical Society*

Bernardsville Post Office, early 1900s, located on Mine Brook Road. It was destroyed by fire in 1930.
Courtesy Bernardsville Public Library

Post Office in Millstone, circa 1905. *Courtesy Hazel Dickinson*

Warrenville Post Office. Daniel Cory was the first postmaster in 1851. Daniel Bornmann was appointed in 1866 and his daughter, Lizzie, held the post from 1882 until 1916. *Courtesy Warren Township Historical Society*

Nordenbrook's General Store and Blackwells Mills Post Office, circa 1910. *Courtesy Franklin Township Public Library*

Store and Post Office, Liberty Corner. *Courtesy The Historical Society of the Somerset Hills*

Far Hills Post Office, early 1900s. *Courtesy Clarence Dillon Public Library*

North Plainfield Republican Campaign Headquarters in 1893. The sign on the building promoted the re-election bid of President Benjamin Harrison and Vice President Levi Parsons Morton. Harrison was defeated by Grover Cleveland. *Courtesy North Plainfield Exempt Firemen's Association Museum*

Presidential campaign, Olcott Square, Bernardsville, 1904. Alton B. Parker was running for president. Henry Gassaway Davis was running for vice president. *Courtesy Bernardsville Public Library*

Theodore Roosevelt, May 27, 1912. The former president stumped in Somerville as the Bull Moose party candidate. Greeted enthusiastically at the train station, Teddy shook hands before heading to the courthouse. There he gave a stirring speech on the steps in the typical Roosevelt style. Neither New Jersey nor the rest of America was ready to elect a third-party president.

Courtesy Somerville Public Library

Former President Theodore Roosevelt makes a point during his speech in front of the Somerset County Courthouse.

Courtesy Somerset County Historical Society

Recruiting Station, No. 2, circa 1917. These men were enlisted at the Armory. Company M was the National guard unit based in Somerville. Uniforms were in short supply, which is why some of the men are wearing shirts.

Courtesy Somerville Public Library

Bernards Township militia being drilled for duty. The unit was financed by John Roebling of Bernardsville. The drillmaster was Joseph Dobbs, far right. Until 1924, Bernardsville and Far Hills were part of Bernards Township.

Courtesy The Historical Society of the Somerset Hills

President Warren G. Harding signing the Knox-Porter Resolution in Raritan Borough, marking the official end of World War I. Senator Joseph Frelinghuysen and his daughter are standing on the left. *Courtesy Somerset County Historical Society*

DISASTERS

If there are lingering doubts that Mother Nature is still firmly in charge, note the picture on Page 78 of flooding in Bound Brook, 1897. Replace the horse-drawn wagon with a car, and the rescue rowboat with a motorized police raft, and it could be September, 1999, when Hurricane Floyd raced across Somerset County, overflowing the Raritan River. One hundred and two years later, we are still humbled by nature's occasional fury.

During the early 1900s, when disaster struck Somerset County, it did so with emphasis. Photographs of fire aftermaths on the following pages in some cases depict nothing but a bare spot where a structure once stood. Only the sturdiest stone buildings seemed to withstand complete devastation.

The photos also show that train travel wasn't the relatively safe proposition it is today. In one particularly bad wreck – on the Delaware, Lackawanna and Western line near Far Hills in 1908 – the entire train has jumped the tracks, with many of its mangled cars lying on their sides along the right-of-way.

As always, disaster turned out the entire community. If you weren't helping – as a fireman or doctor or a member of the bucket brigade – you certainly came out to watch major news as it happened.

Clean up and repair of a truss bridge after a flood and ice breakup, Millstone River and the Delaware and Raritan Canal in Rocky Hill. *Courtesy Rocky Hill Community Group*

Parishioners and residents survey the ruins of the Presbyterian Church in Bound Brook destroyed by fire in 1897. *Courtesy Somerset County Historical Society*

Flooding in Bound Brook, 1897. *Courtesy Somerset County Historical Society*

Members of the North Plainfield Fire Department clean up after fire destroyed several North Plainfield buildings in the late 1800s. *Courtesy North Plainfield Exempt Firemen's Association Museum*

Looking from East Millstone to Millstone during the 1903 flood.
Courtesy Hazel Dickinson

Train accident near East Millstone, 1904. *Courtesy Franklin Township Public Library*

Train accident beyond Voorhees Station, 1907. *Courtesy Franklin Township Public Library*

Train wreck near Far Hills, 1908. *Courtesy Clarence Dillon Public Library*

Fire at the Iron Works, Somerville, July 8, 1909. *Courtesy Somerville Public Library*

Aftermath of the Iron Works fire, Somerville, July 8, 1909.
Courtesy Somerville Public Library

The East Millstone fire of 1912 started in a rubber reclaimation factory on October 28. The fire spread across Livingston Avenue to Pace's Hotel and Gerhart's Store and house. Other houses on Market Street also were destroyed.   *Courtesy Franklin Township Public Library*

Aftermath of the East Millstone fire of 1912. *Courtesy Franklin Township Public Library*

One of the many fire apparatuses used to battle the devastating fire of 1912 in East Millstone. *Courtesy Franklin Township Public Library*

The Unionist Gazette newspaper fire in Somerville, 1917. *Courtesy Somerville Public Library*

The Unionist Gazette plant was left a burnt-out shell after the February 1917 fire in Somerville. The fire started during the night and was well underway before the alarm sounded. Linotypes and machinery crashed from the second floor into the cellar of "Association Hall." Fortunately, the tenants living in apartments above the newspaper office were carried down ladders to safety. *Courtesy Somerville Public Library*

Fire at the offices of the Unionist Gazette newspaper in Somerville, 1917. *Courtesy Somerville Public Library*

TRANSPORTATION

Horses, both the biological and iron varieties, were central to early Somerset County's transportation system. In fact, they were the county's transportation system.

And real horses did have lots of advantages over the automobiles of today. They didn't need servicing, could forage for their own food and did not require parallel parking. On the other hand, modern drivers don't have to shovel out their garages every other day, which was the unfortunate case with horse stalls.

But if you really needed to get somewhere in early Somerset County, you hopped on the Iron Horse, a steam-fired, smoke-belching train. If you wanted a day trip to Lake Hopatcong, you could ride the Central Railroad's "Excursion Special." Needed to reach Manhattan quickly, or get to Philadelphia? There were trains for that, too. (It's worth noting that long trips required a real horse to bring you to the railroad station, where you boarded the iron edition.)

Although trains would flourish for decades, the arrival of cars redefined the way we used horses – increasingly for farm and outdoor chores and recreational jaunts. Once our love affair with the automobile began – at first with cars like Reos and Fiats – we never looked back.

A group of ladies out for a buggy ride stops in front of the Zarephath Post Office, circa 1915. *Courtesy Franklin Township Public Library*

Excursion Special to Lake Hopatcong in the 1880s pulled by Engine No. 107, Central Railroad. *Courtesy Somerset County Historical Society*

Maxwell King is the driver of John Wagoner's hearse at Doughty Avenue and Main Street, Somerville, circa 1870. *Courtesy Somerset County Historical Society*

The wife and daughter of Joshua Doughty Sr. entertain friends in a fashionable surrey, Somerville, circa 1892. *Courtesy Somerset County Historical Society*

Peapack Station, circa 1895. *Courtesy The Historical Society of the Somerset Hills*

Neshanic Station, late 1800s. The woman standing in front of the station is Harriet Nazzaro. *Courtesy Somerset County Historical Society*

The original Far Hills Station, late 1800s. *Courtesy Clarence Dillon Public Library*

Belle Mead Station, late 1800s. *Courtesy Somerset County Historical Society*

This horse-drawn carriage on the Bunn Estate in Bernardsville was a typical form of transportation in the late 1800s. *Courtesy Bernardsville Public Library*

Transportation between Rocky Hill, Kingston and Princeton was handled by the Smalley family of Rocky Hill, circa 1900. Edward A. Smalley owned a dairy farm and his carriages took the older children to and from school in Princeton. He also regularly met trains and transported out-of-town baseball teams to and from the games. *Courtesy Rocky Hill Community Group*

Train trestle near Millington, Delaware & Lackawanna, late 1800s. *Courtesy Somerset County Historical Society*

A bustling Bernardsville Station, circa 1900. *Courtesy The Historical Society of the Somerset Hills*

Lackawanna Station, Bernardsville, early 1900s. *Courtesy Clarence Dillon Public Library*

Finderne Station, early 1900s. *Courtesy Somerset County Historical Society*

Raritan Station, early 1900s. *Courtesy Somerville Public Library*

Somerville Station, circa 1900. *Courtesy Somerville Public Library*

Mule tender's barracks, Griggstown Causeway, early 1900s. This building was used by canal construction workers and mule tenders. *Courtesy Franklin Township Public Library*

Cart used to transport limestone, Peapack-Gladstone, circa 1900. *Courtesy Ruth Thomson*

The Bowers in a horse-drawn carriage in front of their home in Warren. One of their grandchildren is holding the dogs. *Courtesy Warren Township Historical Society*

Early horse-drawn buggy near Somerville, circa 1905. *Courtesy Somerville Public Library*

John Howard Voorhees, son of John A. Voorhess of Pleasant Plains, a section of Franklin Township, sits on a wagon used for gathering firewood, 1904. *Courtesy Franklin Township Public Library*

Baggage man William Wyckoff leans out the door as conductor Oliver Swenson (foreground) signals, "All Aboard." The railroad provided direct service to New York via Jersey City. Photo, circa 1905. *Courtesy Franklin Township Public Library*

Gladstone Station, circa 1907. *Courtesy The Historical Society of the Somerset Hills*

Horse-drawn coach on Claremont Road in front of St Bernard's Episcopal Church, Bernardsville, circa 1905. *Courtesy Bernardsville Public Library*

Middlebush Station, circa 1906. *Courtesy Franklin Township Public Library*

Tracks being cleared in East Millstone, circa 1910. *Courtesy Franklin Township Public Library*

Latest model automobiles on Liberty Corner Road, Far Hills, 1910. *Courtesy Clarence Dillon Public Library*

An afternoon automobile ride in East Millstone, circa 1910. *Courtesy Franklin Township Public Library*

Rocky Hill Station, circa 1919. It was located on the east side of the Millstone River across the road from the canal boat-turning basin. Pictured in front of the station is ticket agent John Tilton. *Courtesy Rocky Hill Community Group*

Central New Jersey ten wheelers No. 165 and No. 754 at Raritan. *Courtesy Somerset County Historical Society*

Weston Station near Zarephath, 1910s. This rail line was built originally as the New York and Philadelphia Air Line and ran from North Plainfield to Hillsborough. The station was located just west of Franklin near Weston. *Courtesy Franklin Township Public Library*

A horse-drawn coach was used to take children to school and on Sunday school outings in Warren, circa 1915. *Courtesy Warren Township Historical Society*

RESIDENTIAL

Somerset County's early housing defined as wide a range of styles and breathtaking prices as does today's real estate. Just how breathtaking, you might ask? We refer you to pages 110-111, and the photographs of Blairsden, the chateau-mansion in Peapack-Gladstone that dominates a hillside overlooking Ravine Lake. Or the ivy-covered Bernardsville home of U.S. Sen. John F. Dryden, distinguished by wide balconies, porticos and a five-story tower, on page 113. These, among many others that still grace Somerset County, are showcase residences for any century.

Not all Somerset County residents lived like that. The lion's share of homes fit a family's needs, and no more. Their styles ranged from French Neoclassical to Colonial, Federal, Victorian, Late Georgian, Dutch Colonial and – well, no style at all.

No matter the style, there was a fondness for picket fences, yards dotted with trees and the kind of homeowner's pride that brought families out front to pose at picture-taking time. And while few homes had the kind of ornate gardens displayed at Blairsden, most were surrounded by flowers, shrubs and well-tended lawns.

House on Dumont Road in Far Hills owned by Charlie Todd, 1913. Left to right: Dorothy Rinehart, Alan Rinehart, Alice Todd and Verna Todd. *Courtesy Clarence Dillon Public Library*

Kirch House on the corner of Mount Bethel and Reinman roads. It is Warren's oldest surviving building. The one-room section of this house was built around 1750 and the two-story section dates from around 1800. This home belonged to the Kirch family from 1857 to 1978, and is now owned by Warren Township. It is on the National Register of Historic Places. *Courtesy Warren Township Historical Society*

Duke's Park, Hillsborough Township, late 1800s. *Courtesy Somerset County Historical Society*

Groendyke Farm, Manville. *Courtesy Somerset County Historical Society*

Benbrook House on the east side of Washington Valley Road, near the intersection of Hunter Road, Bridgewater Township, late 1800s. *Courtesy Somerset County Historical Society*

Casenove House, a summer boarding house and sometime flower pip factory, stood on Reinman Road midway between Cory's Brook and Old Stirling Road, South Stirling. The house and its 53 acres were acquired by the Grundel and Cazeneuve families in 1876. This photo seems to indicate this was moving day, circa 1890.
Courtesy Warren Township Historical Society

William and Susan Sutton Moore in an 1890 photo at their new house on Pottersville Road by Herzog's Brook. *Courtesy Clarence Dillon Public Library*

Allan Hooper, his wife Jane and son Arthur are shown on their Franklin Park farm in 1896. *Courtesy Franklin Township Public Library*

Van Horne House, Bound Brook, October 1897. *Courtesy Somerset County Historical Society*

Ralph W. Thomson house, Middlebush, early 1900s. Thomson wrote a history of Franklin Township and an autobiography. *Courtesy Franklin Township Public Library*

Home in Peapack, early 1900s. *Courtesy Clarence Dillon Public Library*

An early 20th-century photo of Blairsden in Peapack-Gladstone showing the mansion's spectacular mountain-top setting. The mansion's grand south façade extends into the landscape through a series of terraces and stairways. Above the orangery, in the center of the photograph, the main terrace overlooks a vista toward Ravine Lake at the base of the mountain. *Courtesy The Historical Society of the Somerset Hills*

Ravine Lake, Peapack-Gladstone, with the Blairsden Estate in the distance. *Courtesy The Historical Society of the Somerset Hills*

Ravine Lake Falls, part of the Blairsden Estate, Peapack-Gladstone. *Courtesy The Historical Society of the Somerset Hills*

Pump station, Blairsden. *Courtesy The Historical Society of the Somerset Hills*

The ornate gardens of the Blairsden Estate in Peapack-Gladstone. *Courtesy The Historical Society of the Somerset Hills*

George Logan house, Franklin Park, 1904. Ella, George's daughter, is on the porch steps. *Courtesy Franklin Township Public Library*

Residence in Far Hills, circa 1906. *Courtesy The Historical Society of the Somerset Hills*

Mrs. VanArsdale's residence, circa 1905. *Courtesy The Historical Society of the Somerset Hills*

Hardscrabble Farm, circa 1905. *Courtesy The Historical Society of the Somerset Hills*

Home of U.S. Senator John F. Dryden, Bernardsville, circa 1905. *Courtesy Clarence Dillon Public Library*

The Old Stone House built by Johannes Moelich in 1752 was centrally located between Far Hills, Peapack and Bedminster. It was owned by General Reeve. Photo circa 1906. *Courtesy The Historical Society of the Somerset Hills*

G.R. Mosle's residence, Peapack-Gladstone, circa 1907. *Courtesy The Historical Society of the Somerset Hills*

William Flomerfelt, a builder of many houses in Far Hills, built this house at Route 202 and Dumont Road for himself in 1910. *Courtesy Clarence Dillon Public Library*

Residence of Dr. William Long, the school and railroad physician, Somerville, circa 1910. *Courtesy Somerville Public Library*

Hunter house on the south side of Washington Valley Road, near Frohlin Drive, Bridgewater Township, circa 1910. *Courtesy Somerset County Historical Society*

House owned by the Davis family, Millstone, circa 1912. *Courtesy Sara Oderwald, Harry and Pamela Heinold*

Wallace House in Somerville was used by George Washington as his headquarters during the winter of 1778-1779. *Courtesy Somerville Public Library*

William F. Parks house, built before 1900 in Far Hills. *Courtesy Clarence Dillon Public Library*

Riverside Stock Farm, Bridgewater, circa 1915. *Courtesy Marian Meyer*

Vanderveer House was visited by George Washington to express his condolences to the family upon the death of Lt. Vanderveer. *Courtesy Somerville Public Library*

Finderne Farm, Bridgewater, circa 1919. *Courtesy Marian Meyer*

RECREATION & CELEBRATION

Somerset County sure loved a parade. And baseball games. For that matter, it loved fox hunts, horse races, field and track events, circuses, football games and carnivals of any stripe. And except for our forebears' tendency to wear dresses and business suits even to recreational events, our love of recreation and celebration has changed very little in a century.

In the Somerset Hills, where fox hunts and polo were early pastimes of consequence, riders and hounds still set off into the countryside – even if it is increasingly pinched by development.

Parades were an early entertainment staple, with firemen forming the procession's backbone and the entire town lining the streets. One casualty of the last century: the parade of animal performers as the circus arrived in town. In 1907, for instance, Main Street in Somerville was cleared of buggies and cars so a string of circus elephants could file slowly past.

While schools fielded football and baseball teams, Somerset County also sported recreational teams of older players who enjoyed traveling among the communities, looking for a good game.

Children couldn't always participate, but they had their moments, especially when the carnival or circus was in town.

Atlantic Terra Cotta Rocky Hill Baseball Team, circa 1919. Left to right, standing: Harry Newhouse, John Sabo, Bill Volk, Manager Dick Young, Jim McCarthy, Ed Carroll, "Fat" Lewis. Seated: Fred White, Mike Kebish, Roy Durling, Wally Volk, Tom Schott, Wilbur Buchanan. The bat boy is unidentified. *Courtesy Rocky Hill Community Group*

Mrs. Charles Pfizer calling the hounds at the Polo Grounds, Bernardsville, early 1900s. *Courtesy Bernardsville Public Library*

Miss Evelyn Schley driving "Pride and Prejudice" at a horse show at the Polo Grounds, Bernardsville, early 1900s. *Courtesy Bernardsville Public Library*

Firemen march down Olcott Avenue in front of the Olcott School, Bernardsville, circa 1905. *Courtesy Bernardsville Public Library*

The Far Hills Athletic Club was formed by Grant B. Schley to offer track and field competition for youths of the area. The first Far Hills games were held Labor Day weekend, 1904. Standing: Emmett Teets and Charlie Todd. Seated: J. Theodore Stratton and John Nevius. Carroll Van Arsdale is in the chair. *Courtesy Clarence Dillon Public Library*

Far Hills-Bedminster Fire Company parade, early 1900s. *Courtesy Clarence Dillon Public Library*

The fire department puts on a demonstration during a July 4 celebration in Bernardsville, 1906. *Courtesy Bernardsville Public Library*

The fire department joins in a celebration in Bernardsville, July 4, 1906. *Courtesy Bernardsville Public Library*

Far Hills delegation to the Fourth of
July parade in Bernardsville, 1906.
Courtesy Clarence Dillon Public Library

Merry-go-round at the Fireman's Carnival, Peapack-Gladstone, circa 1908. *Courtesy The
Historical Society of the Somerset Hills*

Sledding on a winter day in Basking Ridge. *Courtesy The Historical Society of the
Somerset Hills*

The circus came to Somerville in 1907, bringing rides such as the Ferris Wheel. *Courtesy Somerville Public Library*

Elephants march down Main Street, Somerville, 1907. Somerville was on the main circus railway circuit and Barnum and Bailey's Circus was among those that pitched tents at West End. *Courtesy Somerville Public Library*

The circus in Somerville ran for ten days in July 1907. It featured many popular sideshows for children, such as the Punch and Judy marionette show. *Courtesy Somerville Public Library*

Labor Day track meet at Far Hills Fair Grounds, September 1913. Those known: Don Page, standing in the background, Milton Dillon, sitting to his left, and Father Langon, standing to the right in a dark suit with a straw hat. *Courtesy Clarence Dillon Public Library*

Far Hills Athletic Club Track meet at the fairgrounds in 1910. *Courtesy Clarence Dillon Public Library*

Track meet at the Far Hills Fairgrounds, 1910. *Courtesy Clarence Dillon Public Library*

Early Somerville baseball team. *Courtesy Somerville Public Library*

The Rocky Hill baseball team played neighboring towns such as Hopewell, Kingston and Griggstown. *Courtesy Rocky Hill Community Group*

May Pole celebration at Far Hills Polo Field for children from Basking Ridge, Liberty Corner, Bernardsville and Far Hills schools. *Courtesy The Historical Society of the Somerset Hills*

Far Hills baseball team in 1913. Left to right, standing: Herbert Long, pitcher, William Van Doren, Gideon Scott, Ellis Dow, David Neil and Elwood Little. Seated: Irving Frost, Tom Glover, Richard Seals and William Sueter. *Courtesy Clarence Dillon Public Library*

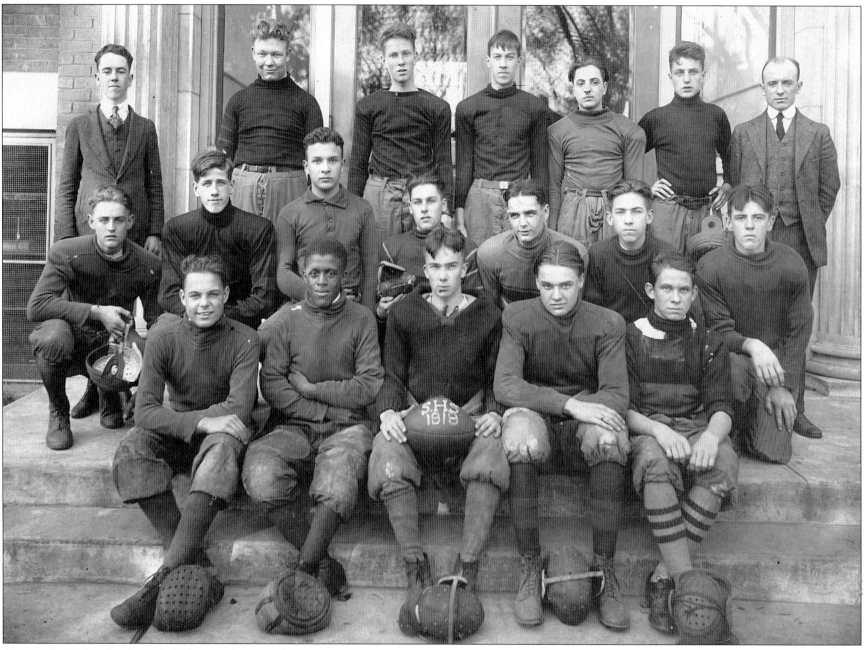

Somerville High School Football Team and soon-to-be county champions, 1919. The team posed in front of Elementary School No. 2. Principal Billy Holbert (far right) and athletic instructor Jim Nash (standing left) were the coaches. The school supplied the team with knickers; however, the boys had to supply their own jerseys. The helmets were leather and without padding. *Courtesy Somerville Public Library*